# EXTREME SPORTS
# SKATEBOARDING

by Tracy Vonder Brink

## Ideas for Parents and Teachers

Pogo Books let children practice reading informational text while introducing them to nonfiction features such as headings, labels, sidebars, maps, and diagrams, as well as a table of contents, glossary, and index.

Carefully leveled text with a strong photo match offers early fluent readers the support they need to succeed.

### Before Reading
- "Walk" through the book and point out the various nonfiction features. Ask the student what purpose each feature serves.
- Look at the glossary together. Read and discuss the words.

### Read the Book
- Have the child read the book independently.
- Invite them to list questions that arise from reading.

### After Reading
- Discuss the child's questions. Talk about how they might find answers to those questions.
- Prompt the child to think more. Ask: Would you like to try skateboarding? Why or why not?

---

Pogo Books are published by Jump!
5357 Penn Avenue South
Minneapolis, MN 55419
www.jumplibrary.com

Copyright © 2025 Jump! International copyright reserved in all countries. No part of this book may be reproduced in any form without written permission from the publisher.

Library of Congress Cataloging-in-Publication Data

Names: Vonder Brink, Tracy, author.
Title: Skateboarding / by Tracy Vonder Brink.
Description: Minneapolis, MN: Jump!, Inc., 2025.
Series: Extreme sports | Includes index.
Audience: Ages 7-10
Identifiers: LCCN 2024032062 (print)
LCCN 2024032063 (ebook)
ISBN 9798892136396 (hardcover)
ISBN 9798892136402 (paperback)
ISBN 9798892136419 (ebook)
Subjects: LCSH: Skateboarding–Juvenile literature.
Classification: LCC GV859.8 .V66 2025 (print)
LCC GV859.8 (ebook)
DDC 796.22–dc23/eng/20240710
LC record available at https://lccn.loc.gov/2024032062
LC ebook record available at https://lccn.loc.gov/2024032063

Editor: Alyssa Sorenson
Designer: Molly Ballanger

Photo Credits: A.RICARDO/Shutterstock, cover; Kong Ding Chek/iStock, 1; kongsky/Shutterstock, 3; Luciano Santandreu/Shutterstock, 4; kornnphoto/Shutterstock, 5; Marc Dufresne/iStock, 6-7; Cavan Images Micro/SuperStock, 8-9; lzf/iStock, 10; Diamond Dogs/iStock, 11; mimagephotography/Shutterstock, 12-13; Luka Banda/iStock, 14-15; BluIz60/iStock, 16; Ulrik Pedersen/DeFodi Images/Getty, 17; Ric Tapia/Icon Sportswire/Getty, 18-19; Sean M. Haffey/Getty, 20-21; xiaorui/Shutterstock, 23.

Printed in the United States of America at Corporate Graphics in North Mankato, Minnesota.

# TABLE OF CONTENTS

**CHAPTER 1**
Skateboarding Basics................................4

**CHAPTER 2**
Street Style................................10

**CHAPTER 3**
Park Tricks................................16

**ACTIVITIES & TOOLS**
Try This!................................22
Glossary................................23
Index................................24
To Learn More................................24

# CHAPTER 1
# SKATEBOARDING BASICS

A skateboarder speeds up a ramp. He twists in the air! How? **Physics** helps him do tricks.

Before learning tricks, skaters must know the basics. They bend their knees. Why? This lowers their **center of gravity**. It helps them balance on their skateboards.

CHAPTER 1

To start moving, a skater keeps one foot on the board. The other foot pushes off the ground. The board moves! Why? Every action has an equal and opposite **reaction**. When a skater pushes against the ground, the ground pushes back. This **force** rolls the skateboard forward.

### DID YOU KNOW?

A skater pushes with their **dominant** foot. Why? It is what feels natural!

CHAPTER 1

Skaters put grip tape on their board's **deck**. The tape is rough like sandpaper. It causes **friction** between shoes and the deck. The shoes grip better. This helps skaters do tricks!

grip tape

CHAPTER 1

# TAKE A LOOK!

What are the parts of a skateboard? Take a look!

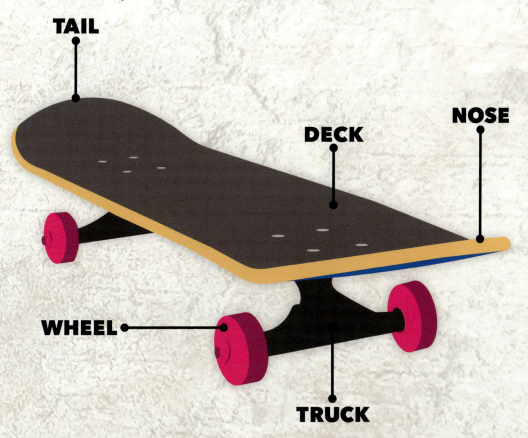

CHAPTER 1   9

# CHAPTER 2
# STREET STYLE

Street is a skateboarding style. Street skaters do tricks in public places.

10  CHAPTER 2

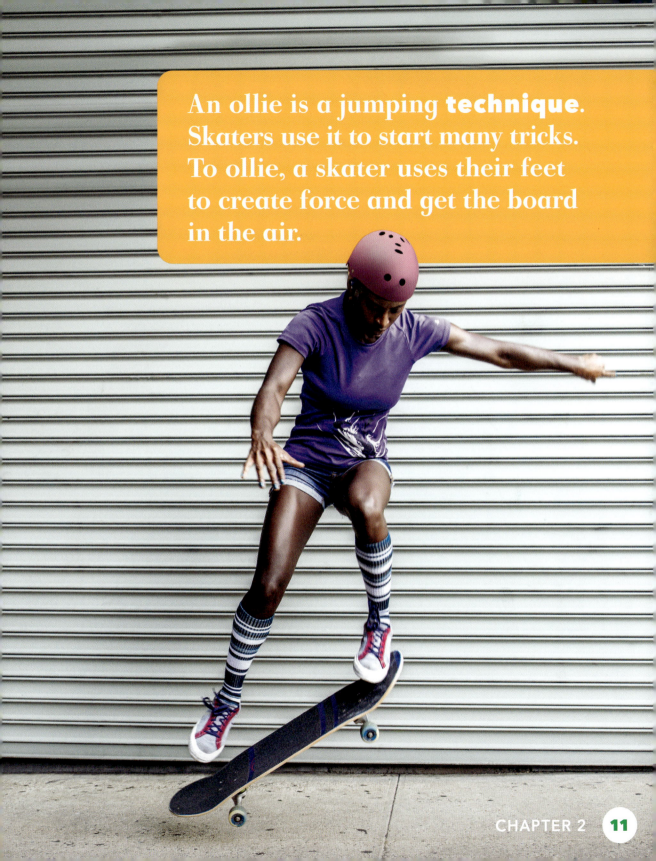

An ollie is a jumping **technique**. Skaters use it to start many tricks. To ollie, a skater uses their feet to create force and get the board in the air.

CHAPTER 2　11

A skater starts with an ollie. Then they use force to **rotate** the board. They do a kickflip!

CHAPTER 2

# TAKE A LOOK!

How is a kickflip done? Take a look!

❶ **The skater starts with an ollie. Their back foot pushes the tail down. The board's nose goes up.**

❷ **The force of the tail hitting the ground pushes the board up. The skater drags their front foot up the board. Friction lifts the board higher.**

❸ **The skater drags their foot off the board. As they do this, they flick the nose with their toes. The force rotates the board.**

❹ **The board flips once in the air. When the deck is upright, the skater places both feet on it.**

❺ **Gravity pulls the board down. The skater lands the kickflip!**

CHAPTER 2    13

Grinding is another trick. To grind, the board lands on the edge of a rail, curb, or bench. The **truck** slides on it. Some skaters put wax on the rail, curb, or bench. Why? This reduces friction. The truck slides easier.

> **DID YOU KNOW?**
>
> Skateboards need hard wheels to do tricks. Why? Harder wheels cause less friction. They slide more. This makes tricks easier.

CHAPTER 2

# CHAPTER 3
# PARK TRICKS

Park is another style. Skaters do tricks on ramps and rails at skate parks.

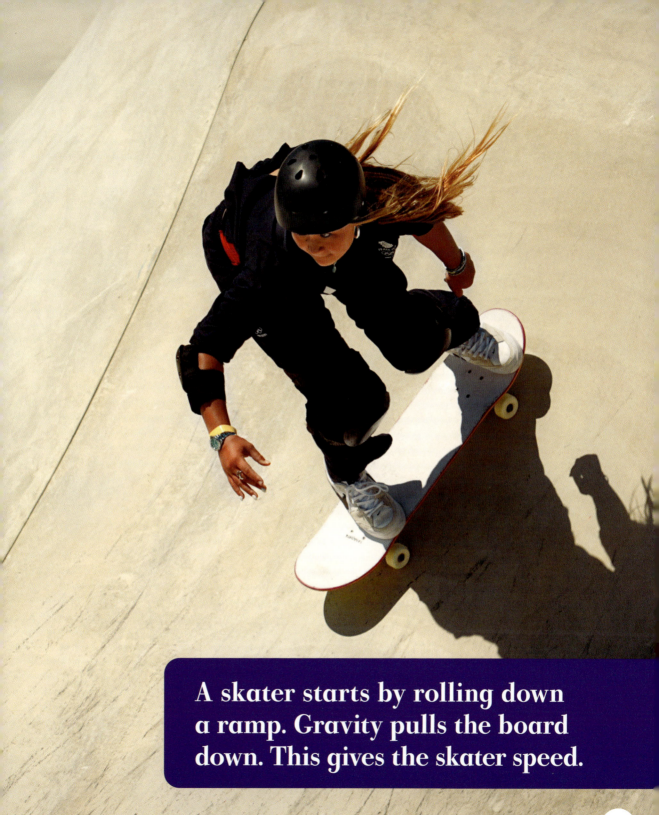

A skater starts by rolling down a ramp. Gravity pulls the board down. This gives the skater speed.

CHAPTER 3 17

A half-pipe is a ramp. It is curved on both ends. Zooming down one side gives a skater **momentum** to roll up the other side.

Skaters **pump** to go even faster. To pump, a skater crouches as the board reaches the bottom. The skater straightens as they start up the other side. Changing their center of gravity builds speed. More speed gives the skater more momentum. They send their board into the air!

## DID YOU KNOW?

The best skaters go to the Olympics and the X Games. They win with skateboard science!

half-pipe

CHAPTER 3 19

CHAPTER 3

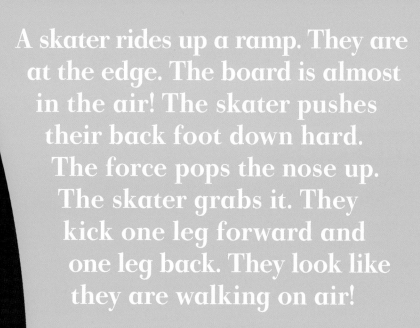

A skater rides up a ramp. They are at the edge. The board is almost in the air! The skater pushes their back foot down hard. The force pops the nose up. The skater grabs it. They kick one leg forward and one leg back. They look like they are walking on air!

Skateboarding takes a lot of practice. But with the right physics knowledge, you can do fun tricks!

# ACTIVITIES & TOOLS

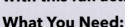

### FRICTION TEST

**Explore how friction works with this fun activity!**

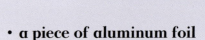

**What You Need:**

- toy car
- cereal box
- a piece of cardboard
- hand towel
- a piece of aluminum foil
- a piece of bubble wrap
- 4 sticky notes
- pencil

1. Write "cardboard," "towel," "foil," and "bubble wrap" on your sticky notes.
2. Put the cereal box on a table or hard floor. Lay it on its side.
3. Rest one edge of the cardboard on the box to form a ramp.
4. Set the toy car at the top of the ramp. Let it go.
5. Mark the spot where the car stops with the "cardboard" label.
6. Put the towel over the cardboard. Let the car go. Mark the spot where the car stops with the "towel" label.
7. Repeat with the bubble wrap and aluminum foil.
8. Compare where the four labels are. Which surface allowed the car to go farthest? Why do you think that is?

# GLOSSARY

**center of gravity:** The point on an object at which half of its weight is on one side and half is on the other.

**deck:** A skateboard's wooden platform.

**dominant:** A person's natural preference for one side of the body, as in a dominant foot.

**force:** Something that causes an object to move or change its speed or direction.

**friction:** The force that slows down objects when they rub against each other.

**gravity:** The force that pulls things toward the center of Earth and keeps them from floating away.

**momentum:** The force or speed something gains as it moves.

**physics:** The science that deals with matter, energy, and their interactions.

**pump:** A skateboarding technique in which a change in body position helps the skater gain speed.

**reaction:** An action in response to something.

**rotate:** To turn around a center point.

**technique:** A method or way of doing something that requires skill.

**truck:** A metal part underneath a skateboard that hold the wheels.

ACTIVITIES & TOOLS

# INDEX

balance 5
center of gravity 5, 18
deck 8, 9, 13
force 6, 11, 12, 13, 21
friction 8, 13, 15
gravity 13, 17
grinding 15
grip tape 8
half-pipe 18
kickflip 12, 13
momentum 18
ollie 11, 12, 13

Olympics 18
physics 4, 21
pump 18
ramp 4, 16, 17, 18, 21
rotate 12, 13
skate parks 16
street 10
technique 11
tricks 4, 5, 8, 10, 11, 15, 16, 21
truck 9, 15
wax 15
X Games 18

# TO LEARN MORE

Finding more information is as easy as 1, 2, 3.
① Go to www.factsurfer.com
② Enter "skateboarding" into the search box.
③ Choose your book to see a list of websites.